Cats

of the National Trust

AMY FELDMAN

First published in the United Kingdom in 2018 by
National Trust Books
43 Great Ormond Street
London WC1N 3HZ
An imprint of Pavilion Books Company Ltd

ISBN: 9781911358367

A CIP catalogue record for this book is available
from the British Library.

25 24 23 22 21 20 19 18
10 9 8 7 6 5 4 3 2 1

Reproduction by Colourdepth, UK
Printed by Toppan Leefung Printing Ltd, China.

This book can be ordered direct from the publisher at the website:
www.pavilionbooks.com, or try your local bookshop.

Kittens photographed
by Chambré Hardman
(see page 7).

Cats

of the National Trust

AMY FELDMAN

National Trust

INTRODUCTION

As they well know, domestic cats have been revered throughout history. The Ancient Egyptians believed them to be sacred and harshly punished those who hurt or killed them. There was a bit of a blip in Europe during the Middle Ages and 15th–18th centuries, when cats were associated with witchcraft and burned alive as a result, but nowadays they're back on top.

If you're reading this you probably agree that cats are pretty special creatures. But what exactly is it about them that we love so much? Why do we put up with their insouciance, their demands, or indeed an attention-seeking puss draping itself over a keyboard (frequently pressing the 'delete' key) as we try to write a book?

I'm not the first person to ponder this question – and not even the first person connected to the National Trust to have done so. Back in 1949, Christabel, Lady Aberconway of Bodnant Garden, Conwy, wrote her compendium of ailurophiles, *A Dictionary of Cat Lovers*, to better understand why some love, and others loathe, cats (see page 23). Playwright Bernard Shaw of Shaw's Corner, Hertfordshire had an answer: 'One understands the possibility of cat worship better when looking at them.' (Stanley Weintraub, 1989)

As their popularity on social media demonstrates, cats are undeniably attractive and amusing to look at. But having written this book, I'd argue it's their personalities – their individual quirks, loves and fears – that make cats so endearing. I've learned of rescue kittens brought in to properties as mousers who have become valued and beloved members of staff. The pets of live-in staff that have carved out their own roles in the team. Many stories are historical, captured in the diaries and snapshots of families who used to live in National Trust properties – including, of course, Christabel Aberconway who, 60 years after writing her *Dictionary*, has become an entry in our own book of cats and cat lovers.

While each cat I've learned about has been unique, they have one thing in common: getting to know them has been a joy. People at each property talked lovingly of their cats. Many told of moggies that have become as photographed as the garden, how visitors will request information about them as frequently as they do the history of their house, or directions to the café and toilets.

For cats bring us laughter, and friendship – and the occasional mouse. This book is a celebration of these enchanting creatures, and of the people who serve them.

The Pet Photographer:

EDWARD CHAMBRÉ HARDMAN

59 Rodney Street, Liverpool

Jupiter, one of Chambré Hardman's subjects, quizzically cocking his head.

When he died in 1988, Edward Chambré Hardman left an archive of more than 200,000 images. He photographed army nurses and captains, professors and reverends and actresses on the brink of successful stage careers. He documented the forgotten corners and everyday life of Liverpool, the town in which he ran his photography studio with his wife Margaret. (Margaret was also a photographer, but was predominantly responsible for running the business.) And he lovingly captured people's pets.

Whether photographing them outdoors, in a studio or at the owner's home, Edward tried to depict his animal subjects acting naturally: a tabby sitting upright in a wicker basket; kittens lapping a saucer of milk (see page 2); a black cat tangling a tape measure. A portrait by Margaret features Stripey, a handsome tabby, celebrating its sixteenth birthday. Cats appear in Edward's landscape photographs too, outside cottages and on pavements, bringing life to street scenes.

Indeed from the volume of cat and dog portraits – some of which were exhibited and one even used on the cover of *Cheshire Life* in 1938 – it seems we have always been fascinated by photos of pets.

The American Beauty:

CHANI

A La Ronde, Devon

When Chani the Maine Coon moved to A La Ronde in 2006, she became the latest in a long line of fascinating females to live in the 16-sided house.

It was first built in the 1790s for two cousins, Jane and Mary Parminter, who intended it to be inherited only by kinswomen (though this wish wasn't always honoured). In the mid-twentieth century it was home to cat-loving sisters, Stella and Margaret Tudor. A photograph of 'Blackie', signed by Stella, remains at A La Ronde and when the house was passed on it came complete with 'BBC' (Big Black Cat), who is now buried in the bee garden.

Chani's favourite activities include promenading along the perimeter path, playing hide and seek in the hay meadow and basking on the 'mounting steps' in the early evening. Wherever she is, she'll make sure you know she's there: she greets staff and visitors with her head, and becomes very vocal if you're not doing as she wishes. Be sure to watch her as she sashays: the fur on her hind legs makes it look as if she is wearing feathers.

Chani poses in the grounds of A La Ronde.

XX DYNASTY
1200-1100 BC.

The Feline Deity:

BASTET

Anglesey Abbey, Cambridgeshire

Anglesey Abbey's bronze statue, with patinated red, green and black marble base; most cat figures are represented in this seated position.

Bastet is the goddess of home, domesticity, women's secrets, fertility and childbirth – and cats. Originally represented as a woman with a lion's head, Bastet was one of the most popular Ancient Egyptian gods. Ancient Egyptian women were regarded highly and enjoyed almost equal rights to men, so any god that protected them was considered important by everyone – after all, if she wasn't looking after you, she was protecting your mother or wife, sister or daughter. Each year, in the ancient city of Bubastis, a festival was held in her honour.

The Ancient Egyptians also revered cats in part because they helped rid the home of pests, including cobras. Cats belonging to royalty might eat from their owners' plates, and amulets of cats and litters of kittens were popular new years' gifts.

Dating from 750–250BC, the bronze statue of Bastet at Anglesey Abbey, which depicts the goddess as a seated domestic cat, is the oldest item in the property's collection.

The Bold Adventurer:
HENRY

Arlington Court,
Devon

When the National Trust created their list of '50 Things to Do Before You're 11¾', they had humans in mind, but that didn't put off Henry. The ginger and white cat has already ticked off almost half of the challenges on the list, including tree climbing, den building, pond dipping, birdwatching and creating wild art.

Despite only having been with the Trust since 2014, Henry has already gained experience at two National Trust properties. His first posting was at Dyrham Park, South Gloucestershire and this was where he embarked on his first challenge. He completed 19 activities before he was 18 months old, including tracking a wild animal – keeping a close eye on Dyrham's eponymous deer.

Henry later moved to Arlington Court in Devon with his owner, Kate, where he's developed a taste for clotted cream. He's also made a new feline friend, Lola, and the pair can often be spotted outside causing mischief. The two cats may also be seen play fighting, but they tend to make up with a cuddle in the evening. Lola even cleans her stepbrother, making sure he's presentable for the next day's adventuring.

Henry (ginger and white) completing the 50 Things activity 'Climb a tree' with his new friend Lola.

The Hungry Gardener:
SCRAP

Attingham Park,
Shropshire

The gardeners who grow the produce in Attingham Park's eighteenth-century Walled Garden have an unusual member of their team: midnight-black Scrap.

Born to a feral cat in Attingham's orchard, Scrap has lived in the Walled Garden for most of her life and takes her role of protecting the produce from mice and rabbits very seriously. She also finds time to entertain visitors, arranging herself on the bench in front of the garden bothy to catch their attention during summer, while in winter she heads inside to warm herself in front of the crackling log burner, or relaxes in pools of sunlight in the glasshouses. But even attention-loving Scrap sometimes needs a break and her shiny black coat provides the perfect camouflage when she disappears into the flower-beds.

It's a good thing Scrap is good at her job because she's not perfectly behaved: a typical National Trust employee, she has a penchant for cakes and biscuits, and will try to steal them from volunteers at break time – as the gardening team reveals: 'We can never leave anything out uncovered because Scrap will eat the lot.'

Scrap relaxing on her seat at break time.

The Good, the Bad and the Lofty:

GREY CAT, TOMMY AND BELLA

Baddesley Clinton,
Warwickshire

Grey Cat on
Baddesley Clinton's
main stairs.

The Senior Gardener at Baddesley Clinton has a rather unusual responsibility: keeping Tommy the cat looking presentable – this rogue requires a daily brush before he's ready for work.

Tommy is named after one of Baddesley's former owners, Thomas Ferrers-Walker (1887–1970). Thomas owned a number of cats during his time at Baddesley, including Black Cat and Black-and-White Cat. But of these, the most devoted was a silver tabby called Grey Cat, who lived to be 21 (1932–52) and followed his owner as he strolled around the estate. Thomas appears to have returned Grey Cat's affection: the feline was depicted in two oil paintings, one featuring Grey Cat alone and the other showing the two together, Grey Cat characteristically watching on as his master is painted in front of the moated mirror. So close were the two, a memorial to Thomas Ferrers-Walker features an engraving of Grey Cat's head.

Tommy the cat was adopted as a kitten from Cats Protection in 2012. He quickly made himself at home in the Baddesley Clinton garden and grounds, accepting attention on his own terms and marking vehicles in the car park.

A year later, Tommy was joined by black-and-white Bella. She too is named after a former resident, Rebecca Dulcibella, who was a member of the 'Quartet', a group who lived at and restored the manor – then in decline – in the late nineteenth century. Bella may seem shy but she loves being made a fuss of – so long as it's not at ground level. She will jump onto a horse box or table before being petted. Her love of heights doesn't end there: Bella can often be found sitting on roofs and Baddesley's stables, and her meals are served on top of a bookshelf.

Bella surveys Baddesley from an apple tree.

The Cat Burglar:
REUBEN

Blickling Estate,
Norfolk

Reuben is always
on the lookout for a
chance to sneak into
the house.

Born to a stray in the gardens at Blickling, Reuben and his sister Meg were quickly adopted by staff. At first, inky Reuben was something of a grouch – while Meg, a tabby, greeted visitors, posed on blankets in the shop and helped sell raffle tickets, Reuben was nowhere to be seen.

But when his sister sadly passed away in 2015, Reuben changed: he's now become a lap cat, observes visitors from his home in a staff flat and enjoys trying to sneak into Blickling's house through the front door. In fact, volunteers have to be alerted when Reuben is prowling the garden, so they can be on the lookout for a cheeky cat burglar!

Christabel Aberconway with her
'personal cat', photographed by
Cecil Beaton. In her memoirs *A
Wiser Woman?* she describes
how in this image she and
the puss were 'listening to a
maddening bird'.

The Scribbler:

CHRISTABEL, LADY ABERCONWAY, AND HER CAT ANTONIA

Bodnant Garden,
Conwy

The idea of writing *A Dictionary of Cat Lovers*
came to Christabel, Lady Aberconway, (1890–1974)
following a train journey in which she and her fellow
passengers embarked upon a debate about cats. In
the book's introduction Christabel writes, 'It
occurred to me, sitting in that darkened train, that if
I could read about people who had liked cats, and
if I could read what they had written about their own
cats, perhaps I might discover why those exquisite,
fastidious and sympathetic animals are either warmly
loved – or loathed.'

Christabel herself loved cats. In 1959, ten years
after the publication of *A Dictionary of Cat Lovers*,
she was interviewed by Daniel Farson for his series
Farson's Guide to the British. When he suggests

> 'If I come back on earth I should like to come back as a British cat because they are so well treated.'

LADY ABERCONWAY'S ITALIAN BUTLER,
Farson's Guide to the British

cats are fickle, she appears outraged: 'Cats are anything but fickle,' she exclaims. 'They are not obedient as dogs are. But they are loyal creatures and affectionate creatures.' Later they discuss how it's uncomplimentary to be compared to a cat, how 'catty' is a negative term. 'There was once a charming photograph of myself and my cat and an Egyptian cat behind me, and it was known as the three cats, and I thought it the most wonderful compliment that I could have,' she responds.

One of Christabel's cats, Antonia (1948–52), is now buried under a yew tree at Bodnant, alongside a commemoration for a fellow feline, Mr Kipps (1943–50). The tradition of cats continues to be upheld with two incumbents, Ginger and Whiskers. They were originally brought in from a rescue centre to keep the mice under control, but 'they quickly discovered the tearoom and the only thing they hunt are titbits from the visitors,' laughs Frances Llewellyn from Bodnant's garden team.

Ginger, one of the two cats in residence at Bodnant, keeps watch over their stomping grounds.

The Cheyne Row Cats:

COLUMBINE AND CO.

Carlyle's House,
London

Thomas Carlyle and
cat in his garden
at Cheyne Row, an
etching by Charles
Oliver Murray after
Helen Allingham.

The letters of Jane Carlyle are witty and absorbing mini comedies and tragedies of daily life. Among the cameos are her pets: cats and dogs and canaries that lived at 24 (then 5) Cheyne Row with Jane and her husband, Thomas, a renowned nineteenth-century philosopher and writer.

In August 1835, a cat reportedly eats one of Jane's pet canaries. In 1850, their black cat Columbine appears in a letter 'written from' the Carlyles' dog, Nero, to Thomas: 'you may know Columbine and I are quite well and play about as usual … Nobody came, but a man for "burial rate"; and my mistress gave him a rowing, because she wasn't going to be buried here at all. Columbine and I don't mind where we are buried.' In July 1852, a new white cat arrives, causing Nero to sulk. Three years later, a stifling summer makes the Carlyles and their cat temperamental: 'It was quite curious to hear the cat squabbling with her cat companions in the garden,' observes Jane.

The Protectors:
DILLY AND NED

Castle Drogo,
Devon

Ned frolicking in
Castle Drogo's
gardens.

In 2014, the gardens at Castle Drogo were suffering: rabbits were eating the herbaceous plants and roses, while voles were stripping bark from yew hedges. The solution: cats. Within a month of the team starting their search, Okehampton Cats Protection had discovered the perfect pusses for the job – three-month-old kittens Dilly and Ned.

Stripy grey Ned is named for Sir Edwin Lutyens (1869–1944), the renowned architect responsible for Drogo, the last castle to be built in England. As with many of his projects, Lutyens worked with a garden designer, in this case George Dillistone, who designed the planting, and from whom black-and-white Dilly gets his name.

Today Dilly and Ned certainly make the most of the architectural garden. They play in the shrubbery and nap in the herbaceous borders, tucked into the base of plants (chosen based on Dillistone's original plans). But it's not all fun and games: Dilly and Ned help to keep away pests, continuing to look after the house and garden created by their namesakes.

'IF YOU CAN REMEMBER
HOW MANY CATS YOU
HAVE, YOU DON'T
HAVE ENOUGH.'

ANONYMOUS

The Allies'
Cat
**CHURCHILL
AND HIS
CATS**

Chartwell, Kent

Churchill bends to
stroke Blackie the cat
during his meeting
with President
Roosevelt on the
HMS *Prince of Wales*.

In August 1941, Sir Winston Churchill met
President Roosevelt aboard HMS *Prince of Wales*.
During the visit, Churchill bent to stroke the
ship's cat, Blackie. The moment was preserved in a
photograph, and Blackie was rechristened 'Churchill'.

Churchill was undeniably an ailurophile and he and
his wife Clementine owned many cats. These included
Mickey, a tabby that caused a commotion while
Churchill was on the phone to his Lord Chancellor.
During the call, Mickey began to play with the
telephone cord, causing Sir Winston to exclaim,
'Get off the line, you fool!' Realising his error, Sir
Winston quickly assured the Chancellor, 'Not you!'

There was also ginger Tango, who kept Sir Winston
company at dinner while Clementine was away; big
grey Nelson, who chased away the previous feline
incumbent of 10 Downing Street; and Smoky the
annex cat who moped when Churchill was away. But
perhaps the most famous of all Churchill's cats was
Jock, who was given to him on his 88th birthday –
see page 36.

'Study for Breakfast at Chartwell II' by Sir William Nicholson. The painting depicts Sir Winston, wearing his favourite blue boiler suit, Clementine and Tango the cat in the Chartwell Dining Room. This is an abandoned first version of the picture, which was commissioned by friends to celebrate the Churchill's silver wedding in 1933.

In 1962, as a birthday gift from his chief private secretary Sir John 'Jock' Colville, Churchill received a marmalade cat with four white paws and a white bib. Named after the gift-giver, Jock the cat quickly became a favourite of Churchill's: it's said dinner didn't start until Jock was at the table and that he was on Churchill's bed when he passed away.

Jock became so much a part of Chartwell that when the house passed to the National Trust, Churchill's family requested that a marmalade cat with a white bib and four white paws always be in 'comfortable residence'. The Trust honours this request and in March 2014 a seven-month-old kitten made headlines when he was rescued from Croydon Animal Sanctuary to replace his retiring predecessor.

Jock VI is well aware of his importance to Chartwell: some days he poses outside the front door courting attention, while on others he'll refuse to be petted or hide under Lady Churchill's bed. There is one constant: Jock VI is impossible not to love.

Jock VI relaxes on top of the steps leading to Lady Churchill's Rose Garden.

The Royal Successor:
CHARLES

Chastleton,
Oxfordshire

In the library of Chastleton House is a bible once owned by Bishop of London, William Juxon. Juxon was with Charles I at his execution; legend has it that this is the bible from which he read to the King on the scaffold.

Although Charles the cat arrived at Chastleton over 350 years later, in 2005, he was well aware of the royal heritage of both his home and his name. He would walk around full of airs and graces and call loudly to demand dinner, but still found time to greet visitors – albeit in an unorthodox fashion. Being jet black, he blended in perfectly with the Victorian kitchen range, and enjoyed jumping out at unsuspecting guests.

Charles, who passed away in 2017, isn't the first cat to have graced Chastleton. It's said the last private owner, Barbara Clutton-Brock (1912–2005) owned many cats. Indeed, according to her granddaughter, the cats would 'hiss and arch their backs at any unwelcome intruders' (Jewell, 1997). Fortunately the only unwanted guests Charles had to worry about were rodents – and he did an excellent job of deterring them.

Charles on duty at Chastleton.

The Nurse's Companions:

FLORENCE NIGHTINGALE'S MENAGERIE AND THE CLAYDON CATS

Claydon House, Buckinghamshire

It's thought that over the course of her lifetime, Florence Nightingale owned more than 60 cats. They appear in her letters and writings and 'sometimes literally stalk through her papers, leaving a trail of inky paw prints' (Bostridge, 2008).

Among them was a large Persian called Gladstone, Mr Muff (who met his end when accidentally shot by a gamekeeper) and Mr Bismarck, 'the most sensitively affectionate of cats', who was large and white, said to be partial to rice pudding with his five o'clock tea and to have eaten dinner from a plate atop a newspaper laid out like a tablecloth.

Florence's cats also travelled with her, particularly to her sister's home in Buckinghamshire, Claydon House. The first time Florence visited, she wrote to the housekeeper in advance: 'May I bring the cats? They are very clean …'.

The housekeeper must have said yes, for there are stories of Florence bringing her pets to Claydon – and of losing them. In 1885, as they travelled back to London, a Persian kitten, Quiz, jumped from the train carriage window near Watford. Fortunately that

Gus exploring the fallen damson tree.

Charley keeping an eye on the sheep over the wall.

evening, Florence received a telegraph from the Watford Stationmaster: 'Cat found not hurt'.

Quiz wasn't the only cat with a roaming habit: in 1869, Tib was found in the home of Florence's neighbour, who happened to be Lord Lucan, leader of the Charge of the Light Brigade. Although Tib was returned, two others – Joseph and Pickle – went permanently missing. Other tales of disobedient Nightingale cats include females ignoring Florence's carefully selected mates in favour of rough-and-ready 'low toms' from the local mews.

Since 2015, Claydon has been home to former rescue kittens Charley and Gus. Whether they would have been clean enough for Florence we can't say, but we do know they enjoy watching visitors from the window, playing chase, dozing in any warm patch they can find and catching mice.

The Indulger:
CLARENCE

Coleton Fishacre,
Devon

Enchanting Coleton Fishacre was built for Rupert D'Oyly Carte. Taking over his father's businesses, Rupert (1876–1948) was proprietor of London's Savoy Hotel, home of Kaspar the cat.

Since 1898, Savoy superstition has dictated that 13 people shouldn't sit down to dinner together. At first the hotel used staff to increase headcount, but found this created an awkward atmosphere. Then, in 1927, architect Basil Ionides gifted a 2ft (60cm) wooden sculpture of a black cat: Kaspar. To this day Kaspar will join parties of 13, complete with a napkin tied around his neck.

Cross-eyed cat Clarence doesn't live at the Savoy, but in a large polytunnel at Coleton Fishacre. It may not be a five-star hotel, but Clarence, who joined the gardening team in August 2015, still treats it like one. His polytunnel is constantly stocked with food and drink and he spends his days relaxing in the gardens and having his tummy tickled by the gardeners. He's quite elusive, though does occasionally earn his keep by posing for visitors in the flower borders or helping the gardeners with a spot of weeding.

Clarence puts on his most demure pose for the camera.

The Boisterous Bengal:
RUBEUS

Cotehele, Cornwall

In case you were wondering, Rubeus is indeed named after the gamekeeper in the Harry Potter stories, Rubeus Hagrid, and for good reason: both men are proud protectors of their stomping grounds.

However, this is where the similarities end. While Hagrid was an animal-lover, ruthless Rubeus prefers to hunt them. He particularly likes to show off his catches and eat them in front of visitors (Cotehele staff do not condone this behaviour). The brown-spotted Bengal also likes to hunt human food and one of his favourite pastimes is stealing from visitors in the Barn Restaurant (Cotehele staff do not condone this either).

When he's not seeking out something to eat, Rubeus might be found following visitors around the garden, snoozing on a blanket in reception or photobombing. In 2016, he even made an appearance in the Catering Manager's son's prom photographs.

But while Rubeus may be a rapscallion, Cotehele wouldn't be the same without him. As a result, he is being honoured in 'Strands of Time', an embroidery project celebrating the property's history; look out for him in the second panel.

Rubeus prowling through Cotehele's extensive garden.

The Happy Huntress:
ARIEL

Coughton Court,
Warwickshire

The first thing you should know about Ariel is that she isn't named after a Disney princess, so don't expect her to act like one. *Ariel* is Hebrew for 'Lion of God' – much more fitting for this feisty feline.

The spirited tabby moved to Coughton in September 2011; then a seven-week-old kitten, she has grown up exploring its grounds. Although her favourite spot is the Cain Brook, where long grasses provide the perfect mouse-hunting ground, Ariel is known to explore far and wide. She wanders the fern-lined paths in the bog garden, stalks her human family as they walk around the property, and enjoys charging over the lawns and up trees. She's also a skilled hunter, which is appreciated by Coughton's gardeners; less pleasing are the occasions when she parades her catches in front of visitors.

Energetic Ariel isn't always on the go. In winter she's just as happy lounging in front of the blazing open fire and at night she'll curl up on a jute bag at the foot of a bed, dreaming of the next day's catch.

Ariel sunbathes in Coughton's grounds.

The Songsters:
CAT MUSICIANS

Erddig, Wrexham

Cat Musicians, oil painting on canvas, 18th century. The painting is part of the Yorke Collection donated to the National Trust by Philip Yorke III in 1973, which comprised the estate and house with all its contents.

In the sixteenth and seventeenth centuries, the Low Countries – a coastal region in western Europe – became known for a rather unusual art trend. Singerie, which can be traced back to Ancient Egypt, depicts monkeys performing human behaviour. The later Flemish painters showed primates gambling and smoking, sculpting and courting, often wearing quite fashionable (for the time) outfits.

Monkeys were not the only animals to be humanised in this way: bird concerts were also popular, and both Jan Brueghel and David Teniers painted 'mewling concerts' of cats.

Part of the collection at Erddig and painted in the style of Flemish artist David Teniers the Younger (1610–90), *Cat Musicians* features both cats and birds, and even a monkey. Cats gather around a musical score while an owl perches on top, perhaps overseeing the occasion. The monkey can be spotted in the left-hand corner, clutching a clarinet; while its identity isn't completely clear, a nineteenth-century inventory described the then-unnamed painting as 'Monkies and Cats'. Studying the image, one can't help but wonder just how the artist imagined the singing session might have sounded.

The Picture Perfect Persian:

PSYCHE THE PERSIAN CAT

Fenton House,
London

'Psyche', A White Persian Cat by Francis Sartorius, oil painting on canvas (1787).

Domestic cats, and certainly Persians, were still something of a novelty when Psyche was painted in 1787. The breed had not long been imported from France, where it was popular in wealthy households. It's said they arrived in Europe via Italian Pietro della Valle in 1626, who discovered the 'very beautiful species' while on his travels. Back then, Persians had longer noses than the flat-faced cats we know today, but charming Psyche still sports their characteristic, irresistible mounds of white fur.

With his bright blue eyes, Psyche wasn't a typical subject for his painter. Francis Sartorius (1734–1804) was actually a popular sporting artist, well known for his pictures of racehorses. Today his oil painting of Psyche hangs in Fenton House's Green Room, which contains a variety of animal objects, including ceramic hares and dogs, and another Sartorius painting, *A Terrier*.

'IF YOU ARE WORTHY
OF ITS AFFECTION, A CAT
WILL BE YOUR FRIEND,
BUT NEVER YOUR SLAVE.'

[attrib.] THÉOPHILE GAUTIER (1811–72)

The Moggy-Coddled Kitties:

ANGELICA, JACINTHA, PROTEUS AND BENJI

Gibside, Tyne and Wear

The Injured Count by Gillray (c.1786), which portrays Mary Eleanor weaning cats while her son laments.

On the day Sue Adamson, Gibside's Community Kitchen Gardener, started at Gibside, there was also an unexpected arrival in the garden: Benji. The tuxedo cat has lived in the property's greenhouse ever since.

Benji was not the first cat to live with an owner of Gibside. Its most prominent, and most tragic, former resident, Mary Eleanor Bowes (1749–1800) was an ailurophile. The Countess of Strathmore and Kinghorne owned at least three cats, Angelica, Jacintha and Proteus, her 'blessed angels'. It's said she once asserted that she hoped 'never to go to heaven, unless she should meet them there' and left a dinner early to attend a cat's christening.

Some, such as the cartoonist Gillray, unfairly portrayed Mary Eleanor as a mother who preferred her cats to her children, but in reality she was actually separated from her children by her two

Benji spends much of the winter in his comfortably heated greenhouse.

cruel husbands. The second, and most dastardly of these, was Andrew Robinson Stoney. Stoney tricked Mary Eleanor into falling for and marrying him, even using her renowned love of cats to woo her: 'were I Proteus, I would instantly transform myself, to be happy that I was stroked and caressed like them, by you.' In actuality, Stoney did not covet the Countess, but her fortune. After tricking Mary Eleanor into marrying him he imprisoned her, letting Gibside fall to ruin, and intimidated its tenants and estate workers as well as selling many of his bride's assets, including her London home, and much more. Thankfully Mary Eleanor eventually escaped him, but the fate of her cats is unknown.

Fortunately Benji has a happier life, eliciting belly rubs and enjoying his favourite foods (salmon, prawns, the odd vole and brand-name cat food – Benji has expensive taste), while in winter, a heater in the greenhouse keeps him warm. He also enjoys rolling in catmint, often with amusing results – watch out for him racing around the garden, leaping through the birch wigwams, or sitting atop a log seat, king of his castle.

The Celebrities:
CRAIG AND COMMITTEE

Gunby Hall,
Lincolnshire

Committee – or
M'Lady, as her
acquaintances call
her – accepts the
gentle attention
of a fan.

Gunby Hall's two feline residents are the rock stars of the heritage cat world: they've appeared in national magazines and newspapers, have been mentioned on BBC Radio 4 and even made their television debuts on the local evening news. Photographers now visit Gunby specifically to try and get a glimpse of these famous moggies.

Long-haired Craig and tortoiseshell Committee (so-called because, with her haphazard colouring, it looks like she was designed by one) have had to work for their A-list credentials. They have been National Trust cats since 2006, when their former owners moved out of their house on the Gunby Estate. The furry duo didn't want to leave, and decided instead to make themselves at home in Gunby's main house. They soon became valued members of staff: Craig patrolling the grounds and Committee helping on garden tours and greeting guests in the courtyard.

In recent years the pair, who are looked after by Clive Ironmonger and the gardening team, have taken a step back from estate duties. Instead they have embraced social media, happily posing for photographs around their beloved estate. Their modelling talents gained a cult following and – eventually – celebrity status.

The 'Top' Cats:

CAT AND CO.

Hill Top, Cumbria

Visitors to Beatrix Potter's farmhouse might find it looks familiar. *The Tale of Tom Kitten*, the story of a naughty young cat and his ill-fitting blue suit, was partly set in Hill Top's garden.

Hill Top has also been home to numerous real-life cats. Beatrix Potter owned several. In the 1950s, after Hill Top opened to the public, Snowy would explore alongside visitors. In the early 1990s you might have found Blackie snoozing in the kitchen window seat. And in 1993, two four-week-old kittens were discovered in the garden and adopted by Hill Top employees; one, named Tabby after *Tom Kitten*'s Tabitha Twitchit, moved into the farmhouse.

Since 2000, Hill Top has been home to black-and-white Cat. In her younger years, Cat took her role very seriously, greeting guests and happily posing for photographs. Today she prefers to watch the world go by, leaving the work to cheeky twins, Mrs M and Venturesome. These two cats have been residents since 2015 and can usually be found in the garden, lazing on paths or peeping out of the vegetation – just like mischievous Tom Kitten and his sisters.

Cat relaxes in the grounds of Hill Top.

The
Gardeners'
Companions:

'SCRIBBLING
BILLY' AND
TIGGER

Ickworth, Suffolk

Sporting a very fine
moustache, William
Rowles (centre) and
his colleagues look
almost as smart as
the cat.

In the 1900s, Ickworth's Walled Garden was bursting
with produce, cut flowers and, in the glasshouses,
exotic fruits – pineapples and nectarines, peaches and
figs. Every morning the Head Gardener telephoned
Cook so she could choose the fruit and flowers for
that day's dining table, making sure they matched
the colour of the dining service being used.

The 5½ acre (2.2ha) garden was tended by an
army of gardeners, including William Rowles, or
'Scribbling Billy', Foreman Gardener between 1906
and 1911. It appears he had a feline colleague: in a
photograph, a black moggy sips from a dish at the
gardeners' feet.

The Bothy remains a retreat for cats, and is
currently home to Tigger. Guests might spot the
lively Bengal strolling along the wall of the Walled
Garden or climbing trees – he's particularly fond of
the wisteria outside the staff cottage. Tigger also has
a penchant for eating, sleeping and playing with any
piece of string he can find.

The High and Mighty:

SAMSON AND THE KNIGHTSHAYES CATS

Knightshayes, Devon

Don't be surprised if you suddenly see a gargoyle move on the exterior of Knightshayes; it's probably just Samson. The Maine Coon can often be found lounging on the Victorian Gothic house's grotesques or gargoyles, or wandering the roof.

According to his owner, Visitor Experience Manager Alice Morgan-Brown, although Samson is twice the size of the average cat, he 'has about half the confidence and a quarter of the common sense'. This, combined with his penchant for heights, can have interesting results; he has found himself stuck on the roof a number of times. Samson's other hobbies include hunting, watching the recycling men empty bins, dining on tender-stem broccoli and tea, and avoiding vacuum cleaners.

Samson shares his grounds with two fellow cats. Lesser-spotted Luna, a shy moggy, spends most of her time hiding in the shrubbery. Abyssinian Billy keeps the rabbit and squirrel population in check, helping protect the 1,200 plant species in Knightshayes' garden. The jury is out on whether this makes up for his naughtier habits of stealing visitors' sandwiches and breaking into the house when it rains.

Samson pretending to be a gargoyle at Knightshayes.

The Limelight Lovers – and Haters:

MORAG AND THE TALBOTS' CATS

Lacock, Wiltshire

'I'm convinced that if that cat could take selfies we'd have a social media star on our hands,' says Lacock's House and Collections Manager Sonia Jones, of grey-hued tabby Morag. Fittingly for a cat who shares its home with the Fox Talbot Museum of Photography, Morag is always primed for a photo opportunity.

Morag clearly doesn't take after one of Lacock's former residents. Charles Henry Talbot, the son of William Henry Fox Talbot (creator of the earliest surviving photographic negative), was a renowned recluse, but from the letters he received we know that Morag continues a long line of Lacock cats.

In 1893, a 'grumpy cat' was thought to be suffering from mange: 'I am sure the best thing you could do would be to have the matted hair cut off as much as possible and the skin dressed with sulphur and hair oil,' advised Charles' uncle, William Gilchrist-Clark. In 1898, the family were looking to re-home Bunny after she was suspected of 'interfering' with Lacock's chickens, though we don't know if 'poor old Bunny' was the culprit, or ever moved from Lacock. A year later, William's sister, Grace, briefly mentions some different cats: 'I was glad to hear about Stripy. It sounds as if the kittens might be tamed after all.'

Button, Gizmo and Sooty are also sometimes seen in Lacock's Tudor Courtyard, but are less interested in being the centre of attention – a little like Charles Henry Talbot.

Morag relaxes on a bench at Lacock Abbey.

The Meowing Dynasty:

THE ROBARTES AND THEIR PETS

Lanhydrock, Cornwall

A studio portrait of 'King Tom' upon a pair of scales, photographed c.1863 by H. Pointer.

Some of the first traces of the Agar-Robartes of Lanhydrock's love for cats appear in letters sent to a young Thomas Charles in 1854. 'The cats appear very happy and are quite well – they spend most of their time on a wool mat before the kitchen fire,' wrote his nursery maid, Sarah Warsop.

Cats appear in family snapshots as well as formal portraits, both with family members and by themselves. One picture, from c.1863, features a huge tabby, 'King Tom', sitting upon some scales, two yellow bells tied around his neck. In 1890, ten-year-old Everilda sits for photographic portraits; in one image, a tabby sprawls in her lap, in another, a white cat. Fifteen years later she is photographed again, more informally, in the garden, a long-haired puss sitting elegantly upon her knee.

While the cats were clearly beloved by the Agar-Robartes, their staff didn't always share their feelings. One housemaid recalled how cats and dogs had free rein in the house, often leaving 'mess' that the servants had to clean up, and how the cats had to be shooed from the dining table as they would jump up to eat leftovers.

King - Tom

The Farm Cat:
FREDDIE

Lower Halsdon
Farm, Devon

When Andrew and Kate moved to Lower Halsdon Farm in May 2016, they found it came with an unexpected addition: Freddie the cat. Apparently Freddie had been making the farm his second home for years, sleeping in the barns, hunting in the hedgerows and searching the kitchen for bowls of milk.

It seems right that a cat has adopted the tenanted farmhouse. Former owner Stanley Long (1918–2001) turned down a £4 million offer from developers, instead choosing to leave Lower Halsdon to the National Trust, so that the Exmouth community could enjoy it forever. Stanley was a renowned animal lover and hopefully would have approved of Freddie enjoying his generous bequest.

One of Freddie's favourite spots is the Exe Estuary Trail, which passes by the farm's entrance. Here he lies in wait, ready to surprise passing pooches: 'I've seen many a dog start to whimper and cry as they approach a hissing Freddie,' reveal Andrew and Kate.

Freddie shows a softer side when it comes to humans: he loves having his stomach rubbed and rolls on his back at the slightest sign of attention.

Freddie exploring
Lower Halsdon Farm.

The Writers'
Inspiration:

**SNOWDOVE
AND THE
HARDYS**

Max Gate, Dorset

'Hardy showed me the graves of his pets, all overgrown with ivy, their names on the headstones,' wrote E. M. Forster of a visit to Thomas Hardy's home, Max Gate, in 1922. 'Such a dolorous muddle. "This is Snowbell [sic] – she was run over by a train… this is Pella, the same thing happened to her … this is Kitkin, she was cut clean in two … of course we have only buried those pets whose bodies were recovered. Many were never seen again." I could scarcely keep grave – it was so like a caricature of his own novels or poems.' (E. M. Forster, 1985)

'Snowbell' was in fact Snowdove, a white cat remembered in Hardy's 1904 poem 'Last Words to a Dumb Friend'; it's said Hardy even chiselled her name onto her gravestone. Snowdove may be the only Hardy cat with a dedicated poem, but Thomas and his wife Emma owned at least nine while at Max Gate, among them Comfy, Kitsey, Marky, Pella, Tippety, Kiddleywinkempoops – 'Trot' for short – and Cobby, a blue Persian rumoured to have disappeared without a trace following Hardy's death in January 1928. The Max Gate pet cemetery continued to grow long after the Hardys had left, subsequent tenants burying their pets alongside Snowdove and co.

Thomas Hardy with one of his many beloved cats.

75

Hardy and Emma invited their pets to mealtimes, even when they had guests. One such event in 1912 was recalled by poet Sir Henry Newbolt: 'I could hear and see Mrs Hardy giving [W. B.] Yeats much curious information about two very fine cats who sat right and left of her plate on the table itself. Yeats looked like an Eastern Magician overpowered by a Northern Witch.'

Emma was not so much of a writer as her husband, but she did send many letters to newspapers campaigning against animal cruelty and, in 1898, had an article, 'The Egyptian Pet', published in *Animals' Friend*. In it, she implores readers to 'Always give a cat free ingress and egress and attend to his voice, remembering that he has no language but a cry.'

'PET WAS NEVER MOURNED AS YOU, PURRER OF THE SPOTLESS HUE, PLUMY TAIL, AND WISTFUL GAZE WHILE YOU HUMOURED OUR QUEER WAYS.'

THOMAS HARDY, EXTRACT FROM 'LAST WORDS TO A DUMB FRIEND'

a cat purring

The Cat Man:
JOHN LENNON AND HIS MOGGIES

Mendips, Liverpool

The story of John Lennon's lifelong love of cats begins with Elvis. Elvis the cat, that is, who was named after the singer and belonged to John's mother. The moggy surprised everyone when she gave birth to kittens in a cupboard, though the family decided not to change her name.

A few years later, after John had moved into Mendips to live with his Aunt Mimi, who raised him, he rescued a half-Persian ginger stray he'd found in the snow. Tim, as he was christened, lived to be twenty. John also doted on Mimi's other cats, Sam (named after diarist Samuel Pepys) and Tich. It's said that he biked to the fishmonger every day to fetch fish for the moggies and even when travelling the world with The Beatles regularly phoned home to speak to Mimi – whom he affectionately called 'the Cat Woman' – and catch up on his beloved pets.

He went on to own a number of cats of his own, including ten with his first wife, Cynthia, one of which, 'Mimi', was named after his aunt. Many of his cats' names reflect John's reputed wit: Salt and Pepper (allegedly Salt was black and Pepper white), Major and Minor, and 'Jesus', one of the many owned with Cynthia, presumed a sarcastic response to John's controversial 'more popular than Jesus' remark of 1966.

John Lennon, 'A Cat Purring' from the book *Real Love: The Drawings for Sean* by John Lennon.

John Lennon and Yoko Ono with one of their cats.

John and Yoko Ono also owned cats, one of whom, Alice, plunged from the window of a high-rise apartment. 'That was the only time, I think, I ever saw my dad cry,' recalled their son, Sean. In later years there were three further cats, Misha, Sasha and Charo.

John also enjoyed drawing his pets and many of his sketches were published in *Real Love: The Drawings for Sean*. He and Sean often drew together, cats and otherwise, said Yoko Ono. 'The drawings were done in the spirit of laughter … and lots and lots of Jove.'

Lennon may have referred to his Aunt Mimi as 'the Cat Woman' but John Lennon was, undeniably, 'the Cat Man'.

The Pampered Puss:

BALOU

Middlethorpe
Hall, York

Balou plays
with Christmas
decorations at
Middlethorpe Hall.

With 20 acres (8ha) of gardens and parklands to romp in, a luxury spa for tired paws, and open fires for warming up after a long day of hunting, Middlethorpe Hall would be the perfect (or should that be purrfect?) home for distinguished felines – if they had it their way.

Built in 1699, the William and Mary country house is the stomping ground of Balou. This 'larger than life' tabby lives nearby with the hotel's Director and General Manager and is clearly proud of his territory. He keeps the grounds pest-free, often greets guests outside the front entrance, and makes sure his master doesn't do too much overtime by waiting for him outside the door when it is time for his shift to end.

Balou also goes the extra mile to make visitors feel at home. One guest, a well-known television personality, asked permission to take Balou to his room for company. Balou was, of course, happy to oblige and accompanied him for most of the afternoon.

> 'Kind old ladies assure us that cats are often the best judges of character. A cat will always go to a good man, they say'

VIRGINIA WOOLF, *Jacob's Room*

The Bloomsbury Pet:

VIRGINIA WOOLF'S PETS, SAPPHO AND PLUTO

Monk's House, East Sussex

Believed to have been taken at Monk's House in 1947, this photograph features Sappho and Pluto.

When Virginia Woolf received her first pay cheque for a piece of journalism she decided to treat herself: 'I went out a bought a cat – a beautiful cat, a Persian cat.'

The tom was not without its troubles, getting into 'bitter disputes' with neighbours. But this didn't deter Virginia or her husband, Leonard, from owning future pets – they even adopted a marmoset, Mitz, rescued from a junkshop by their friends the Rothschilds. They also owned two more cats, Sappho and Pluto, probably during their tenure at Monk's House.

Virginia's character comes through in her cats' names. Fascinated by astronomy, she and Leonard purchased a telescope in 1930, the year Pluto was discovered. Sappho was an ancient Greek poet, known for her work on love and women, and the love between women – all of interest to Virginia. Virginia said that to know everything about Sappho is not to know much at all; perhaps she also believed that, like many felines, Sappho the cat had mysterious qualities.

The Ladies
who Lunch:

**ELINOR
GLYN,
CANDIDE
AND ZADIG**

Montacute,
Somerset

In *A Dictionary of Cat Lovers*, Christabel, Lady Aberconway observes that those who love cats often resemble them. Aged 16, the fiery-haired, green-eyed, cat-loving romantic novelist Elinor Glyn (1864–1943) was compared to one of the grandest cats of all: a 'Belle Tigresse'.

In 1907, Elinor embarked on a passionate eight-year affair with Lord Curzon, the former Viceroy of India. In 1911, Curzon leased Montacute House in Somerset, an Elizabethan mansion that had fallen into disrepair. He invited Elinor to live with him to help with the renovations and for 18 months she endured freezing temperatures as she knocked Montacute into shape. Curzon repaid her with an engagement announcement in *The Times* – to another woman. Receiving no explanation, Elinor left Montacute and never spoke to him again.

Elinor's own cats certainly resembled their owner: glorious marmalade Persians named Candide and Zadig in tribute to Voltaire. 'They were beautiful, proud, independent creatures of enormous characters and "it", in many ways very like their mistress', wrote Antony Glyn, 'Elinor was devoted to them'. In March 1939, one even accompanied Elinor to a literary lunch where she was guest speaker. Ever-controversial, ever attention-grabbing, Elinor wore 'with fine panache, her huge Persian cat, Candide, asleep round her neck' (Glyn, 1955).

Elinor photographed
with Zadig (left) and
Candida (right) in 1931.

The Old-timer: MURPHY

Mottisfont,
Hampshire

'Resting in the garden's catmint', 'catnaps in the second-hand bookshop' and 'providing photo opportunities for all visitors' are just three of the key duties of the Mottisfont estate cat, a role Murphy has held since 2004.

Murphy's years of experience also enable him to go above and beyond. His role includes crowd control at outdoor-theatre shows, when he has also been known to make impromptu appearances on stage. And to ensure food quality is up to scratch, fearless Murphy thinks nothing of strolling through the audience to test the picnics.

He sometimes goes rogue, though. Mottisfont's House Manager, Sophie West, recalls a particularly rainy day: 'Murphy snuck upstairs to the Lady's Maid's Room to get dry and fell asleep on a chair … He was so still that several visitors thought he was stuffed – until he suddenly moved and gave them the fright of their lives!'

While Murphy isn't planning to leave his post anytime soon, future applicants should note that a Mottisfont cat works for 37.5 hours per week ('not including catering and "deep-sleep" periods'). Additional duties include mouse and rabbit control, night security of the shepherd's hut and purring enthusiastically at visitors.

Majestic Murphy guards Mottisfont.

The Prized Possessions:

THE STRAWS AND THEIR CATS

Mr Straw's
House, Worksop,
Nottinghamshire

William Senior with
kittens, photographed
some time between
1923 and 1932.

Set on suburban Blyth Grove, this Edwardian semi-detached house is a time capsule, the story of an inter-war grocer family: William Straw Sr, his wife Florence and their two sons, William Jr and Walter.

Within are hints of a family who loved cats: a leather collar; postcards of Louis Wain illustrations (1860–1939), an artist renowned for anthropomorphising cats; a box of unused Christmas crackers with cat-shaped labels; Christmas cards featuring felines carolling or curled up by the fire or playing a trumpet; and family photographs showing William Sr, Florence and Walter playing with ginger tabbies. On the wall, a kitten calendar dated 1932 has hung there ever since William Sr passed away in June that same year, the time-capsule house a tribute to him.

On 15 February 1913, Walter entered a kitten into The Worksop Band of Mercy Show of Pets, in which it took third place. This wasn't quite as successful as Walter's previous year's endeavour with his doves, however – they came top of their class.

The Mature Mouser:
FREDDIE

Packwood House,
Warwickshire

The position of Chief Mouser in Packwood's Kitchen Garden is currently held by Freddie, a rescue tabby with a lemur-like ringed tail of white and grey.

Freddie arrived in 2011, then aged six, and quickly settled into the role. The team even kept a scoreboard of his catches, which usually numbered at least two or three a day. Nowadays Freddie's finds are more sporadic, but his presence at least discourages the rodents.

Freddie's hunting may not be consistent, but he's otherwise a creature of habit. Lunch is followed by a dinnertime stalk of the gardener locking up the glasshouses – he knows that once the job is finished it is time for him to be fed. (This tends to be wet food; Freddie's missing a few teeth these days.)

When not munching on mice, Freddie can be found snoozing in the heated glasshouse. You may spot him rolling around in catmint and grasses, or chatting with Packwood's gardeners and grown-up visitors. He also enjoys attention and, if he knows you really well, likes being cradled on his back. What a softie.

Freddie in Packwood's
garden shed.

92

The Aristo-Cats:

THE PECKOVERS' CATS AND ALGERNON

Peckover, Cambridgeshire

Sisters Alexandrina (left) and Anna Jane in the Peckover gardens with their cats, some of which are now commemorated in the garden.

In a sheltered spot of Peckover is a small graveyard: the resting place of many cats (and one dog) lucky enough to have lived here.

The oldest graves date from the early to mid-nineteenth century, to the last generation of Peckovers who lived in the Georgian town house. Here lie Bijou, Zeta and Angel; Pharos, the 'much beloved beautiful tabby'; 'very loving and faithful' Ginger (d.1935) and Marmie, a 'most beautiful and loving orange cat', for whom the Peckovers threw a sixth birthday party. More recently, they have been joined by Mulberry and Damson, both residents during the National Trust's time at the house.

Today Peckover is home to Algernon, or Algie. This thick-coated feline is named after Algernon Peckover, one of two brothers who helped develop much of the surrounding area. Algie is a cuddle-seeker and will climb the gardeners' legs or sit on their laps while they're working in search of attention. But he also has a surprising nemesis: blackbirds. The birds are completely unafraid of him, and he sometimes has to have a minder to stop them tucking into his dinner!

The Great Extravagance:

CAT AND SNAKE SCULPTURE

Powis Castle and Garden, Powys

Arriving at the Castle via the descendants of Robert Clive, 1st Baron Clive (1725–74), the 'Cat and Snake' sculpture is an intriguing item in Powis' collection. Its true age is a mystery: some say it is Roman, dating from the first century BC. Others claim it is later, from the eighteenth century (together with a number of other sculptures at Powis previously believed to be Roman).

Robert Clive discovered the statue in Italy and his excitement about his find is palpable in a letter to his cat-loving wife, Margaret, in which he describes the artwork as 'delightful' and 'exquisitely fine'. If it was Greek or Roman, as Clive believed, it is also very unusual: felines were rarely depicted in art of this era. It is also a high-quality carving, especially as it is made from a type of marble that is very difficult to sculpt.

In his letter Robert Clive worries that the cat is 'out of reach of money'. But determined to acquire the cat for Margaret, he resolved to do so '*Coûte que coûte*' – whatever the cost. The amount he ultimately paid remains unknown.

The marble cat and snake sculpture on display at Powis.

The Lasting Legacy:
BETTY HUSSEY AND HER CATS

Scotney Castle, Kent

John Ward's 1965 oil painting depicts Betty Hussey in middle age, a black cat – possibly one of the many Minous – perched on her lap.

In the grounds of fourteenth-century Scotney Castle is a fountain. On one edge, a stone cat – its collar engraved with the name Minou – lies with its paw dangling over the side, a lazy attempt to catch a fish.

The fountain was commissioned by Elizabeth 'Betty' Hussey. Since moving to Scotney in 1952, Betty had always owned a Burmese cat, each one named Minou (French for 'kitty'). For her ninetieth birthday she sold some of her jewellery to create the fountain in honour of her cats and the pleasure they gave her.

Scotney is also bursting with Betty's feline trinkets and models, fridge magnets and paintings. There are old copies of *Your Cat* magazine, flea treatments and specially made stairs leading to cat flaps. Portraits of Betty feature Minou as prominently as any human family member.

The National Trust did not just inherit inanimate objects. Betty also asked if she could leave her final cat at Scotney, in the Trust's care. So when she passed away in 2006, the Trust became the guardians not only of Scotney, but also of Puss. Puss didn't just break Betty's trend for calling cats 'Minou'; she also wasn't a Burmese but a tortoiseshell.

We don't know how Puss came to Scotney but we do know that, like all of Betty's cats, she was well cared for (some might say spoiled). She slept in a basket atop the piano and even enjoyed dinners there. The Trust had to make a few adjustments to Puss's feeding routine, weaning her from fresh salmon to tinned cat food, and removing the bowl (and basket) from the piano.

Puss still had the run of the house however: she had a basket in the kitchen and dozed on Betty's bed. She became a much-loved feature of Scotney – so much so that, when she passed away in 2015 at the grand age of 19, a number of people attended the scattering of her ashes.

Puss was often found making herself comfortable on Betty's bed.

In honour of Betty the team decided there should always be a female rescue cat at Scotney. Today that is ebony Betsy.

‘CATS HAVE IT ALL –
ADMIRATION, AN ENDLESS
SLEEP, AND COMPANY ONLY
WHEN THEY WANT IT.’

ROD MCKUEN,
Stanyan Street and Other Sorrows

Bernard Shaw's wife,
Charlotte, dozing with
a tabby upon her lap.

The
Playwright's
Pets:

**BERNARD
SHAW**

Shaw's Corner,
Hertfordshire

Bernard Shaw was an animal lover: famously
vegetarian, anti-vivisectionist and described by
his biographer Michael Holroyd as having 'a
fellow-feeling with cats'. He was also a keen
amateur photographer and his images capture
many a moggie. They stroll beneath umbrellas,
stretch on a window ledge and sprawl across his
wife, Charlotte, as she sleeps in Shaw's (temporary,
following foot surgery) wheelchair at Blencathra,
one of their later homes.

'Bunch would pad behind him when he went round the garden, and it would leave the kitchen to sit in the dining room with Shaw because he always put the stove on when it was the least cold. He was kind to Bunch.'

SHAW'S SECRETARY, BLANCHE PATCH (1951)

The photographs also feature Bunch. Bunch belonged to the Shaws' housekeeper, Alice Laden, but this didn't stop Shaw referring to the orange and ginger tom as 'our cat', nor Bunch's ashes from being scattered at Shaw's Corner.

Shaw's love for cats can still be felt at Shaw's Corner: in a ceramic white porcelain cat in the drawing room, its ears pricked and tail curled around its body; until recently, in Socks the cat, known to appear on the veranda during outdoor theatre performances; and in Socks' successor, Molly, a fluffy tabby who greets visitors as they explore the grounds.

Socks enjoying the sunshine in the garden at Shaw's Corner.

The Mystery:
THE CAT'S MONUMENT

Shugborough,
Staffordshire

The origins of Shugborough's Grade II-listed Cat's Monument are a mystery. The flat-faced sculpture may represent a cat that accompanied former resident Admiral George Anson on the HMS *Centurion* as he voyaged around the world from 1740–44. If true, the cat's commemoration isn't so surprising: moggies have been valued ship's crew members since the time of the Ancient Egyptians, acting both as companions and pest control. And if the cat accompanied the Admiral for the whole four years, its survival is remarkable: just 500 of Anson's 1,900 sailors lived to tell the tale.

The other theory is that the statue commemorates a Persian cat, Khouli Khan, who belonged to Admiral Anson's older brother, Thomas. Thomas Anson, a long-standing MP, is said to have loved cats and kept Persians for many years. He also had a herd of curly-horned Corsican goats and the presence of the goat's heads at the base of the statue gives credence to this theory.

The Cat's Monument,
Shugborough Estate.

The Tarot Cat:

SNUFFLES

Smallhythe
Place, Kent

Snuffles appears in this 1919 oil painting of Smallhythe by Clare Atwood. At the time, Atwood, Edy Craig (second from right) and Christabel Marshall (first on the left) were living in a *ménage à trois*, a relationship that lasted from 1916 until Edy Craig's death in 1947. Ellen Terry is also featured – the last on the right.

The daughter of renowned Victorian actress Ellen Terry (see page 112), Edy Craig was a theatre director, costume designer and early pioneer of the women's suffrage movement in England. Her cat has a more unusual claim to fame: Snuffles (or Snuffy), is said to have been an inspiration for the popular 1910 Waite-Smith deck of Tarot cards.

The deck was created by artist Pamela Colman-Smith. She was a regular visitor to Smallhythe, where Edy lived with her mother, and it is said that she painted scenes from the cottage into the cards, that either Edy or Ellen is the Queen of Wands, and Snuffles is the black cat depicted throughout. The truth of this is unknown, but the tale has immortalised Edy's pet. Snuffles has since become a common name for black cats on Tarot cards.

Edy and her cats appear to have had a strong relationship and in February 1923, it was even mentioned in the *London Evening News*. The paper reported that Edy's cat was pining while she was away in Egypt working on the silent film *Fires of Fate*.

The Thespian:

ELLEN TERRY AND BOO BOO

Smallhythe, Kent

At Smallhythe, there is a small wicker basket with two small windows, a door, a domed lid and a handle. This is no ordinary shopping basket: it was specially made for Dame Ellen Terry (1847–1928). The renowned Victorian actress used it to carry her fluffy cat, Boo Boo, between her London home and country cottage, Smallhythe.

As striking as her cat, Dame Ellen was a leading actress of her time; she played some of the greatest leading ladies in Shakespeare as well as many other classic roles. As Virginia Woolf once wrote: 'She filled the stage and all the other actors were put out, as electric lights are put out in the sun.'

In 1892, she also famously began 'paper courtship' with a fellow cat-lover, the then relatively unknown Bernard Shaw (see page 104). Despite only living 20 minutes from one another, the pair avoided meeting for fear that it would spoil their playful letter-writing. When they did eventually meet, Ellen remarked that 'he was quite unlike what I had imagined from his letters' – though quite what she meant by this, we don't know.

Ellen Terry photographed with Boo Boo, c1918–20.

The Model Cat:

CHARLES PAGET WADE'S WOODEN CAT

Snowshill Manor and Gardens, Gloucestershire

It is said that Snowshill's last resident, Charles Paget Wade, once confided to architect Sir Edwin Lutyens that he 'had never grown up'. Apparently his friend, Professor Albert Richardson agreed. The Professor felt Wade needed company at Snowshill, but wasn't responsible enough to look after a 'real' pet. He presented Wade with a life-sized wooden cat painted with black markings.

Eccentric Charles purchased Snowshill in 1919, when it was essentially a ruin. He laid out the gardens and restored the house, which he filled with over twenty thousand items, from penny farthings to Samurai armour and Balinese masks. Charles lived in a cottage across the courtyard from the manor. Here he was accompanied by his wistful-looking wooden cat, which stood on a rug by the fire, an empty food bowl in front of him. Staff have even reported finding dead mice next to the wooden cat – a ghostly mystery or former feline resident 'Tino' bringing his friend a present?

Professor Richardson may not have believed that Charles could take care of a living cat, but he certainly looked after his wooden one, replacing its whiskers every year. This is perhaps less surprising when you remember his motto: *Nequid pereat*, 'let nothing perish'.

The wooden cat with his empty bowl.

The Bankers' Cats:

THE HOARES AND THOMASINA

Stourhead, Wiltshire

The story of the Hoares of Stourhead's cats is sporadic and mysterious, but we think it begins around the 1770s, with a formal portrait of a young child, either Peter Richard or Henry Merrick Hoare. The oil painting, by renowned society portrait artist William Hoare of Bath, RA (1707–92), also features an elegant grey cat upon the subject's lap.

Fast forward 100 years, and a cat makes a cameo appearance in the diary of Augusta Hoare. On 15th February 1883, she recalls a visit from 'Frank', who 'brought me a cat, "Fanny"'. Yet just a few months later, on 1 June, she writes, quite matter-of-factly, 'darling … (cat) died … Went with Mary to a meeting at Gros House for Soldiers' Institute.' Whether this was the same cat she was given by Frank is unknown.

More recently Stourhead has been adopted by Thomasina. Named by a resident member of Stourhead's donor family, the moggy has made herself at home in their flat as well as that of the House Manager, and can often be seen on the first floor windowsills, begging to be let in.

The pastel portrait of Peter Richard or Henry Merrick Hoare by William Hoare of Bath, c 1770–92.

> '*The independence of the cat, the wilfulness of his comings in and his goings out, is a reproach to dull humans who cannot but resent it.*'

LADY MANDER, *CATegories*

The CATegorical Cat-lover:

THE CATS OF LADY MANDER

Wightwick Manor and Gardens, West Midlands

Rosalie, Lady Mander met Ricardo of Pimlico (Ricky), at Pimlico Tube Station. He was a stray cat and she adopted him. Together they would travel from Lady Mander's London flat to her William Morris-filled home, Wightwick Manor. Lady Mander would buy a ham sandwich for the journey: she ate the bread and butter while Ricky snaffled the ham.

Ricky wasn't Lady Mander's only cat. Miss Tabby Cat received a dedication in Rosalie's 1981 anthology of feline-focused writings, *CATegories*: 'Without whom sitting Sphinx-like on the desk or playing "with sportive grace", kittenish on the keys, this book would have been finished much sooner.' Miss Tabby also appears in a photo with Lady Mander on the jacket.

Lady Mander and her cats may no longer be at Wightwick but their presence is felt strongly: through the trinkets she collected and was given by Wightwick's volunteers; through new feline residents Sybil and Sam who prowl the grounds on the lookout for mice; and through the cat cushions placed on the chairs, indicating to weary visitors where they can sit.

Lady Mander with Ricky the cat, c 1980.

The House Cat and the Garden Cat:
GINA AND GINGER

Wimpole,
Cambridgeshire

Tucked away on the library shelves at Wimpole Hall is a red cloth book with three gold cats embossed on the spine: Christabel Aberconway's *A Dictionary of Cat Lovers* (see page 23). Inside is a personal inscription to a twentieth-century Wimpole resident, the daughter of Rudyard Kipling: 'For Elsie Bambridge – who loves beautiful things, including cats.'

We don't know much more about Elsie's love of cats, but it seems like she probably would have appreciated that 60 years later her house would be home to two attractive felines.

Gina the tabby has lived at Wimpole all her life: abandoned as a kitten in 2001, she was taken in by the Shop Manager. By making herself at home on the shelves of Wimpole's shop, she has unwittingly become a 'must-see' and has been photographed by local journalists and painted by artists. Like many of the National Trust's most precious collections, it's a case of 'look, but please don't touch' – while Gina loves people, she doesn't appreciate being stroked while sleeping.

Lionesque Ginger on the other hand is more likely to be seen wandering outside or snoozing in the sunshine. In winter, you might see him keeping warm by sitting on car bonnets, leaving muddy footprints and tufts of fur as he goes – a different kind of a souvenir from a day out.

Ginger is usually found exploring Wimpole's grounds.

The Horticaturist:
GERTRUDE JEKYLL AND HER CATS

Cats were a prominent feature at the home of Arts and Crafts garden designer Gertrude Jekyll (1843–1932). According to her nephew Francis Jekyll, 'If [a visitor] was lucky enough to find a chair unoccupied, he was soon to discover that Gertrude's attention … was divided into three parts, one for himself, one for the tea-things and one for Pinkleboy or Tittlebait.' (Jekyll, 1934). Those are just two of the cats Jekyll owned; others included Mittens, Octavius, Tavy and Toozle.

Jekyll didn't live in a National Trust property, but helped create them: her repertoire of designs includes Barrington Court, Somerset and Lindisfarne Castle, Northumberland. The fact that she had 'four or five' cats living with her at any one time – and often as many as eight – clearly didn't distract her; she worked on 400 gardens and wrote over 1,000 articles during her lifetime. She also found the time to draw cats, including 'plans' of s reminiscent of garden designs and an oil painting of her own cat, *Thomas in the Character of Puss in Boots* (1869), now on display at Godalming Museum, Surrey.

Gertrude Jekyll in 1923, seated on her camp stool in the Spring Garden at Munstead Wood.

BIBLIOGRAPHY

Aberconway, C., *A Dictionary of Cat Lovers, XV Century* BC–*XX Century* AD (Michael Joseph, 1949).

Bostridge, M., *Florence Nightingale: The Woman and Her Legend* (Viking, 2008).

Day, C., *Larry, the Chief Mouser and other Official Cats* (Pitkin Publishing, 2016).

Deezen, E., *John Lennon was a Crazy Cat Lady* (Retrieved from *Mental Floss*, 17 November 2017 http://mentalfloss.com/article/29696/john-lennon-was-crazy-cat-lady).

England, M., 'A Spider in the Bath': The Young Thomas Charles Agar-Robartes, *Lanhydrock House Journal* No. 6, pp. 15–22, Winter 2006.

Forster, E. M., *Selected Letters of E. M. Forster 1921–1970, Volume Two* (Harvard University Press, 1985).

Glueckstein, F., '"Cats Look Down on You ..." Churchill's Feline Menagerie', *Finest Hour* 139, 50, 2008.

Glyn, A., *Elinor Glyn: A Biography* (Hutchinson, 1968 revised edition).

Henderson, A., *George Bernard Shaw: His Life and Works* (Stewart Kidd Co. Company, 1911).

London Evening News, 'The Sad Cat – and Why', February 1919.

Jekyll, Francis, *Gertrude Jekyll: A Memoir* (Jonathan Cape, 1934)

Jewell, S. *To the Manor Born, then the National Trust Took Over* (Retrieved from *The Independent*, 17 November 2017 http://www.independent.co.uk/life-style/to-the-manor-born-then-the-national-trust-took-over-1234973.html).

Leith, S., *Dead Pets* (Canongate Books Ltd, 2005).

Mander, R., *CATegories* (George Weidenfeld and Nicholson Limited, 1981).

McConnell, A., *Cats in the Lacock Archive* (Retrieved from *Lacock Unlocked*, 17 November 2017, http://www.wshc.eu/lacock/lacock-unlocked/people/item/cats-in-the-lacock-archive.html).

Patch, B., *Thirty Years with GBS* (Victor Gollancz, 1951).

Weintraub, Stanley ed., *Bernard Shaw on the London Art Scene 1885–1950* (Pennyslvania State University Press, 1989).

Walker-Meikle, K. *The Cat Book* (Bloomsbury, 2015).

PICTURE CREDITS

INDEX

ABOUT THE AUTHOR

Amy Feldman is an Editor at the National Trust. She is the author of the National Trust guidebooks to Brockhampton Estate, Townend and Tudor Merchant's House, and also contributed to the Bath Skyline guidebook. She currently owns one cat, a mischievous black-and-white moggy named Puffin.

ACKNOWLEDGEMENTS

This book would not have been possible without the enthusiasm of the National Trust staff and volunteers who took the time to talk to me about their cats past and present, undertook research, checked drafts and even performed cat photo shoots. Thank you all so very much.

A huge thank you also to the many external people who were so kind in assisting with research, including Andrew and Kate at Lower Halsdon Farm, Sue Baxter at the Claydon House Trust, Daisy May Bodewes, Holly Carter-Chappell at the Florence Nightingale Museum, Lionel Chatard at Middlethorpe Hall, Helen Gibson and the team at Dorset County Museum, Dr Jane Hamlett, Jonas Herbsman at Music Law, Louise Hodgson, Luke Kelly, Alexandra K McConnell at Wiltshire and Swindon Archives, Judith Tankard and Zoe Wilcox at the British Library.

Many thanks, too, to the team at National Trust Books and Pavilion who indulged my love of cats and gave me the opportunity to write this book, and for their support throughout, particularly Katie Bond, Claire Masset, Peter Taylor and Kristy Richardson.

Also to those who spent many an hour in a car with me, talking through and encouraging the book and for your boundless enthusiasm – you know who you are.

And finally, my eternal gratitude to John, without whose support this book would never have been written (well, at least not to deadline!).